MULE

10TH ANNIVERSARY EDITION

WITH NEW POEMS BY THE AUTHOR AND AN INTRODUCTION BY VICTORIA CHANG

MULE

SHANE MCCRAE

Cleveland State University Poetry Center
Cleveland, Ohio

10TH ANNIVERSARY EDITION

Printed in the United States of America
Printed on acid-free paper

ISBN 978-1-7348167-4-7

Second edition

23 22 21 20 19 5 4 3 2 1

This book is published by the Cleveland State University Poetry Center, 2121 Euclid Avenue, Cleveland, Ohio 44115-2214 www.csuohio.edu/poetrycenter and is distributed by SPD / Small Press Distribution, Inc. www.spdbooks.org.

Cover image: Horgan Jr., John. "Fifty African American men guide mule pulled cultivators through cotton field, 1891." Everett Collection.
Mule: 10th Anniversary Edition was designed and typeset by Amy Freels in Stone Print with Copperplate display.

A catalog record for this title is available from the Library of Congress.

to my family

Contents

8 (NEW POEMS)

Afterword

Breaking Language Towards Beauty: On Shane McCrae's *Mule*

Victoria Chang

I still remember the first time I opened Shane McCrae's first book of poems, *Mule.* This was 2011—a turbulent year. I remember the earthquake and subsequent tsunami in Japan, the earthquake in New Zealand, the riots in England, and so much more obliteration, sorrow, and fires.

My father had a devastating stroke in 2009 and language would be one of his many losses. My children were still very young and I wasn't able to find the time or the mental space to write, and I had recently left a long-term job due to a challenging boss.

But when I opened McCrae's book and began reading, suddenly a new kind of exciting turbulence emerged—a new language appeared, one that I had never experienced before. Where did this language emerge from—Berryman, Hopkins, Shakespeare, Plath? I couldn't pinpoint its influence because McCrae's language, combinations of language, and sheer disruptive energy within that language were and are wholly his own.

After I finished McCrae's book, his ringing repetition and charged syntax lived inside my mind for weeks. One morning, the phrase *the boss the boss the boss* repeated and I began to write something that would eventually become my third book of poems, *The Boss.* In essence, seeing McCrae's new language gave me the permission to make my own music, however unconventional it might be. Seeing McCrae's language disrupted my own creative paralysis.

The second poem in *Mule,* "In No Place," introduced me to McCrae's language, where language is woven into intricate tapestries and then fractured into new combinations and possible meanings:

And we divorced in any anyhow / But sudden anyhow

but hurry we / Divorced in sudden hurry the affair / Become the main thing don't

want to be mar- / ried still become the main thing anyhow

Already sit and don't go out

McCrae covers a broad swath of subjects in his poems, such as parenthood, childhood, marriage/divorce, race, faith, and history. None of these subjects are uncommon in poetry, but it's McCrae's language and his unique use of form that are completely memorable and singular.

Some poets and I are currently reading Wallace Stevens's poem "Sunday Morning" together, and while reading McCrae's book, I can't help but think of Stevens's line, "Death is the mother of beauty." McCrae's work stems from trouble and death—death of a marriage, death of a grandmother's brain, death of faith both in identity and religion. But out of these multitudes of death comes beauty, a beauty through language.

Later in Stevens's poem, he rephrases the same line as: "Death is the mother of beauty, mystical, / Within whose burning bosom we devise / Our earthly mothers waiting, sleeplessly." McCrae's poems evoke a kind of mysticism where the reader becomes entranced in a liminal spiritual state of betweenness. This liminal space is where the speaker sits as well. A mule is the offspring of a donkey and a horse but it is wholly neither, as is explained in the first poem of the "Mulatto" series. It is in this state of mystical betweenness where tension exists and where beauty arrives.

Throughout *Mule,* McCrae's poems deploy caesuras, slashes, a lack of punctuation, repetition, and line breaks, as if to attempt to control the rhythms in his poems, but in many ways, the attempts have the opposite effects. These choices unravel McCrae's formal poems (which are often, but not always, iambic sonnets with 70 beats) and suddenly his poems become new and fresh. The result is a powerful tension between form and fracture, between structure and anti-structure.

Every poem in this book follows patterns and simultaneously unravels them, as if one were knitting a scarf, thinking it was finally finished, only to look back and see that a child had been unraveling the scarf the entire time. What's left is a smattering of yarn with the intensity of having once been some other form, if only for a second.

In the poem "Internal Horses," the speaker is in the midst of a divorce, while he is watching his autistic son play at the park:

> As we divorced   Nicholas rode
>
> internal horses   / And watching him
>
> from the bench at the edge of the park / In wildflowers
>
> him in wildflowers him in fields / Of wildflowers him in fields   on playgrounds which
>
> Blossom from the ground
>
> and then the ground
>
> Must be covered over   with foam with bark
>
> It was and it was possible
>
>
> To love him just enough   to sit there watch- / ing not enough   for us to stay together

Not more enough   than us

If we had put our ears to the ground

we might have heard the horses / Carrying him our son away

the sound   carried away and al- /so back   both   both together

Not running from and not   running to us

This poem appears in the third section of the book, a section that delves into the world of the speaker's autistic son. Although there are threads in subject matter that overlap across sections of this book, each section of the book hinges on a different subject, such as the son's autism, the speaker's grandmother, marriage, divorce, race, childhood, and faith.

Language and subject matter link and morph in interesting ways throughout the collection. "Internal Horses," for example, begins with the phrase "As we divorced," echoing the repeated phrase from the first section of the book, "And we divorced," while countering the phrase "We married" that is repeated throughout the second and third sections of the book. The poem's opening with an "As" versus an "And" implies a lack of a temporal quality of grief and endings, as if to say that neither a marriage nor a divorce happens with one event—both are streaks that span time and place.

This poem, like all the poems in this book, is roughly iambic: "As we divorced" can be scanned as u/u/ (unstressed, stressed, unstressed, stressed). The longer line in the poem: "To love him just enough   to sit there watch- / ing not enough   for us to stay together" is perfectly iambic (sometimes lines are even perfectly iambic pentameter).

But like all the poems in this book, the iambs in this poem are severed by caesuras, dashes, slashes, and sometimes line breaks. Throughout the book, even words are broken into pieces. All of these formal elements, combined with the lack of punctuation, tug and pull at each other, evoking a sense of aching while reading. The tension arises from the speaker's desire for control and regularity, but his utter inability to control anything.

In this poem, the son is riding "internal horses," implying a private life within the son's mind. This internal world mirrors the speaker's own privacy, as the speaker is not invited into the son's mind or even into the park. The speaker is at the "edge of the park" in his own thoughts, nearly strangled by his own gaze and inability to enter the "wildflowers" or the fields where the son is located. The speaker cannot enter the space of the son not only because of the son's autism, but because of all the other fraying edges of the speaker's marriage. The estrangement that the speaker feels is multitudinous—across time, space, events, and people.

The caesuras, dashes, and line breaks mirror the fissures of the speaker's life as well. Nothing is certain anymore. At the transition between the first and second stanzas, there is a major crevasse, both literally and figuratively with the double return. In all of the poems in the book, the spacing appears to be double-spacing. There are gaps everywhere:

> It was and it was possible
>
>
> To love him just enough   to sit there watch- / ing not enough   for us to stay together
>
> Not more enough   than us

The poem repeats "It was" as if to insist that loving the son is enough, as if insisting can lead to actuality. But then the speaker negates his own thinking: "to sit there watch- /ing enough," mimicking how the mind (and heart) can wish and unwish simultaneously, believe and unbelieve at once.

The final stanza begins with an "If": "If we had put our ears to the ground/ we might have heard the horses." Ultimately, the speaker didn't put his ear to the ground and thus was not able to hear the horses, which is a figurative gesture towards failure, towards giving up. The speaker's self-blame is evident here, as is guilt and shame, all themes explored in this book.

With this tenth anniversary edition of *Mule,* McCrae has added 11 poems that were not originally in the first edition. When reading these poems, I imagine that every book of poems must have at least a few poems that, for some reason or other, were not chosen for the final book. In reading McCrae's additional poems, I continue to marvel at his imagination: "We married in one hundred dirty hooves" begins the poem "The Math." The poem's utter comfort in the play of language is what I noticed about the book when I first read it a decade ago: "we married in / The math so probably twenty-six may- / be twenty-seven animals."

The poem "My Grandmother Married a White Supremacist and Became a White Supremacist" begins: "We filed the papers at a hydrant my / Grandmother painted over over and / Over again the hydrant in her front / Yard ..." McCrae's gift for the unexpected metaphor repeats again and again in the same way his words repeat throughout the book. We also begin to see the themes of race, history, and injustice appearing in these early poems, themes which McCrae would continue to explore in his subsequent books over the next decade.

All the poems in *Mule* push forward, then back, forward again, and then back through syntax, the line, form, and repetition, so that ultimately what the reader feels is something akin to an unsettling religious incantation. In McCrae's marvelous world of language, everything is certain, then nothing is certain, and back again, and everywhere in between.

"Imagine // welcoming the wound," McCrae writes in his frontispiece poem, "The Cardinal Is The Marriage Bird." McCrae not only acquiesces to the wound in *Mule,* but he revises the wound through language, and in the process, we are in the midst of beauty. I hope that a new generation of readers, through this tenth anniversary edition, will be able to experience the skillful contradictions within McCrae's language, and be opened up and broken in the same way that I was when I first read this stunning and singular book.

MULE

The Cardinal Is the Marriage Bird

The cardinal is the marriage bird / And flies a flash of dusk

becomes   forgets becomes / Again the body

of the cardinal in the sunlight in the day   / Imagine

otherwise the cardinal in the room

The sunlight in the room in the day / The sunlight

on the snow the snow   like frosted glass   / The cardinal in the snow

as clear as if it were   on the inside side of the window

And not in the world the cardinal is

The marriage bird and flies   in the sunlight on the snow / Between the sunlight and the snow

a shadow on the snow but still / The sunlight on the snow

imagine otherwise

The cardinal on the windowsill

And flies

a flash of shadow and the cardinal is the shadow bird / A flash of wound   the wound

bird evergreen to evergreen

Wound leaping evergreen to evergreen / Imagine

welcoming the wound

1

In No Place

And we divorced in any anyhow / But sudden anyhow
but hurry we   / Divorced in sudden   hurry the affair / Become the main thing don't
want to be mar- / ried still become the main thing anyhow
Already sit and don't go out

in an- / y sudden every sudden thing   and we
In any hurry turn to salt and break   / The farther I
run far from you   the less / I feel my own body
and turn to salt   / and break   and hurry have
to get now back / Home to Chicago every sudden thing / Marries

already there's no money left

And we divorced in anyhow the eyes

Except the eyes eyes   turn to limestone in their sockets and the eyes

go also numb / And any hurry hurries home   and once

I had a lover and a lover and a fine

Lover I had a lover and she was mine

As lost as sudden suddenly

The woods behind my house are trees

In no place

every time I touch you I feel less

Of my own body fingertips and wrists   / Elbows and shoulders strange

to feel the numb- / ness as a tingling as an extra burst

Of life to signal something dying

hur- / ry the affair become   the main thing hur-

ry any anyhow become your home

Is anyhow your home and have you ever

had another / And wander through the woods   and make the forts / Made

of stripped trees   my forts / As sure as my

body is mine as sure

The trees would either way

bend but to strip them first

Is mine if I am in it is / And have I have I ever ever have

Is anyhow my home and have I ever / And have I ever every sudden thing

In every sudden thing I look for you

And that is how I look for you

Bend but to strip them

ladders hanging from the trees

But first we had to choose the tree   and clear the hives / From the tree

but first we had to climb

The Survives

And we divorced in the survives   and O

It was a comedy   and first you ever slept with me

And marry me and marry me and O

How fat I used to be

The mountains were not mountains and

The snow we drove through sudden and

The mountains were not mountains every   *and* an *if*   as in

You if you loved me   if you loved me

we / Pulled over   and the snow was in the trees

As if the snow and not the trees

were living were / The living thing   the branches did not change

The snow fell   from the branches in

The wind and snow

the twigs by the road were dry enough to burn

It does not matter if we change

In the Garden of the Ghosts of the Garden

And we divorced in water in a gar-

den in the pond in the garden in the pond

Up to our ankles in the mud and neck-

deep in the water   and we stood in the water

We held our arms above our heads for for-

ty days supported by the water and

Weighed down by the water   and we didn't drink

For fear that we would leave ourselves no water

To stand in   and we didn't piss   for fear that

We would pollute the water and have no

Water to drink stood   forty days in the pond

Nothing was left   of the garden but the pond

No house no flowers   no fence no bushes no

Road to where a house would be   the garden

And you   and me   we felt our bones disin-

tegrating in the sun   and freezing back

Together wrong   in the night   and the night sky
Was one-half solid white   and one-half sol-
id black   and gave no light   and we each   morn-
ing woke   to different bodies frozen back
Together wrong inside   for forty days
We stood in the water   in the mud   in the hole
In the garden of the ghosts   of the garden wait-
ing to be exiled from the garden as
Even the water disappeared   the last
Trace of the garden   and by the forty-first
Day it was gone   still   hands in the air   we wait-
ed there   for anyone to punish us

2

WON'T

Won't you yes   marry me O Mary pray / O May we may

to the marriage of imped-

iments admit two minds   O Mary May

I have distinct and often wondered memories

For sixteen hours and for

twenty-four hours / I've waited for the day

O Mary as / If waiting were the day

for thirty years

If waiting was the day   I've wasted my whole life

O Mary won't O Mary   won't you yes   / Or give me such a no as says you're lying

O Mary won't you O May lie to me / O Mary

give me such a yes as says you won't

[We married in a thorax]

We married in a thorax no idea
What kind of bug a flying bug we mar-
ried off the ground   we married in the air
We married over a trailer park by the sea
At sundown   by the sea and somewhere west
A western state at the edge of the west the night
Becoming morning facing   west the night
Becoming something unfamiliar as
The night was unfamiliar where we lay
The night before the day we married in
A thorax hovering no   judge no min-
ister no pilot and no guide no way
Out the wings drowning out   the sea our voic-
es no vows just   the living body's noise

Sightseeing

We married on a sightseeing train the pas- / sengers each

spoke a different language none

Our language and   the farther the train traveled

From home the fewer of

each other's words / We understood

through jungles and

through des- / erts and   through forests and through farmland from

Home through the fewer of   to none

we traveled   / From the station to the hotel at the lake

And from the wedding to the honeymoon / To bed

we traveled on the train to bed

Each with a different word for *bed*

and in / Our dreams saw things   we couldn't when we woke / Describe

that might have been the same things our / Hands made the same

strange animals in the air

Horses Running Fast

We married in an open field a wide

And open field a field of wild and run- / ning

horses wide a field of horses run- / ning through

we married in an open wide

Running and full   of horses open

field / And in we married in   and in we mar- / ried in in

one direction they the hors- / es they

disguised the wind as horses in the wind / The horses running

fast in one / Direction

as the horses running through   / The horses as the horses run- / ning through

and each of us as me and you / As horses running fast

In one direction and

no animal outruns its past

[We married on a battlefield]

We married on a battlefield the war a
War of attrition slow attrition so
Slow we built houses on the field brick hous-
es and the enemy built houses of
Loose sticks and mud   we raised our children there the
Enemy had no children they had cows
They raised their cowherds there they raised their no
Children on the battlefield   and some wore hooves
Hollowed-out hooves as shoes and some of their
No children drank from the hooves we did-
n't let   our children mix with their no chil-
dren   didn't let our children drink their milk
We watched our children   everything we did
We did to keep our children safe for the war

[We married on a speeding train]

We married on a speeding train the roof
Fighting with knives a speeding train we were
Fighting each other   stabbing through the roof
The windows but   where were the passengers
Stabbing each other full of holes   but no
Blood and no bones the knives slipped through our bod-
ies and we didn't lose   our balance though
We lunged and we were stabbed we were not dead
But we were dying though   we lunged and we
Were stabbed and didn't bleed and fought on the roof
And didn't fall we fought and didn't see
It what was really killing us   and if
We had we wouldn't   *even if*   have stopped
Stabbing each other   half of love is hope

3

After the Diagnosis

We married in the boy we thought he would

Be honey cinnamon and was the man

A genius   artist mathematician hus-

band father beautiful and is he was

Always so beautiful our son our map

Of us and nobody we knew the sun

A compass in the east   the moon a cres-

cent moon and monsters   dragons barely vis-

ible in the wide sea   near the tall ships

Both on the map and in the world but not

The same monsters on the map and in the world

And not the same   world on the map and in

The world the same sea in the world   and in

The world the monsters stretch from coast to coast

[We married in his belly]

We married in his belly our son's bel-

ly our autistic son we married in

His ghost the son we had   the son we have

His ghost we didn't know him in his bel-

ly no   we did not know him not the son

We had we do not know the son we have

We've read about him sometimes in the books

The Have-You-Seen-This-Child books all night we

Read all night searching for our son   but dai-

ly parts of the son we have disintegrate

And disappear   we don't know who we're look-

ing for we married in his belly   we

Would know it if we saw it now no way

To see it now no way to see inside

Recovery

We married in recovery our son's

Almost immediate recovery

After his diagnosis in the hope

Almost immediate an intake spe-

cialist she didn't know him anyone

Though could have said the same kind things and we

Would have believed her married in the hope

He would escape in the hope we would escape

His autism married for a year at the end

Of spring and comes the summer spring but hot-

ter one year later and he isn't get-

ting better O it's one year later and

We've never seen that specialist again

Again O once you're in you're always in

[We married in a taxi]

We married in a taxi in Chica-

go mid-   November in the long wind blowing

Our son has autism married in the back

Seat of a taxi slipping in the wind

We'll never have   you said another child

On Michigan and on our left the lake

The long white shadow of the lake in the blowing

Wind and what happens   you asked when we die

Who will take care of him the taxi slip-

ping in the wind and on our right the Mir-

acle   and on our right the Miracle

Mile ending on our right no miracles

Cheaper hotels but   he can't sleep when we're

Not there you said   how will he get to sleep

The Boy Calls Twilight

The boy calls twilight   *little dark* the night
Big dark and smiles at the moon on the wall   the boy
Rocking himself to sleep his head against
The padding on the bars   until he falls
Over and sleeps   and if he wakes in the night
The boy   his head against the padding he
Rocks in the big dark little rocks and soft-
er once   and softer twice   until he falls
The boy he slumps   against the bars of the crib
Falls over falls asleep   and wakes in the lit-
tle dark the morning   little dark the lit-
tle dark through the window little   blue on the crib
And on the moon   which does not glow in the light
The little light   the moon is for the night

Internal Horses

As we divorced   Nicholas rode

internal horses   / And watching him

from the bench at the edge of the park / In wildflowers

him in wildflowers him in fields / Of wildflowers him in fields   on playgrounds which

Blossom from the ground

and then the ground

Must be covered over   with foam with bark

It was and it was possible

To love him just enough   to sit there watch- / ing not enough   for us to stay together

Not more enough   than us

If we had put our ears to the ground

we might have heard the horses / Carrying him our son away

the sound   carried away and al- /so back   both   both together

Not running from and not   running to us

A Dancer There

And we divorced in there a dancer there / A town with no flat surfaces
no park- / ing lots his bike in the trunk   no tennis courts / And when I don't
prepare myself to see

Myself and see   suddenly my reflection I
Feel sick   and suddenly my body   suddenly   / And he
one day our son one day / Who looked so much like me he does-

n't anymore   and we in there / Are dancers
and I see us separating / In him

his face that was my face / Becoming yours   / His nose still mine
I see us separating
He rides his bike in circles on a hill

The ache in his legs whenever he turns back

He Turns a Corner

And we divorced in every time my heart / He turns a corner stops   he turns
And I can't see him anymore   / And he

autistic children run away / And he
I pick him up from school he runs
Out of the room ahead of me   and down the hall
I pick him up from day care   but we call it school   / And he
will never be with kids like this again
Kids who aren't like him

And every time he runs   ahead of me away   / And down the hall
to the corner and
around / The corner
and he disappears

Ahead of me and I can't make him

stop   or turn / Runs

laughing through the door   into the dark

[We married in the front yard]

We married in the front yard watch-

ing our son disappear   our two-year-old

Son Nicholas we watched him disappear

Gesture by gesture   word by word his au-

tism slowly   erasing him he couldn't catch

A ball   he could have caught the ball before

Forgot   the word for ball we didn't know

Which mattered more   the action or the word

Which disappearing part was more   impor-

tant more   our son which part   to hold and which

Part to let go we said the word and rolled

The ball again we said   the word and rolled

The ball we rolled the ball and we said   *catch*

He held his arms out   and embraced the air

4

Singing

We were   back then a problem

now we are / A problem

but we're not the same

problem we were / Unsatisfied we wanted what they had

and now

We want what we had then we didn't know

We had it then we didn't know how far

We'd have to go how   much we'd lose

taking it where

To find them they   were everywhere   but hid- / den they were

part of everywhere

and then we found

Paths to their houses burned their houses down / The city

burning our own

homes but they had gone / Already left

the thing behind we burned

Our fingers we   burned the skin off

our fingertips / Pulling it from the fire we burned our lips

Kissing it burned our tongues

singing to the thing we burned

That's Entertainment

White half the white half   mule the black half black   / But more

pleasing to either eye more hav-

ing neither but the black half eye   more hav- / ing neither

which which half

the bigger half // Is it the smaller half   the bigger half

Which half the horse   which half half human being   / And which which

half is neither of these things / The bigger half

is twice as big   and can't

Be measured

but the smaller half is twice as small / Who wouldn't love an animal

Cheaper to kill than heal

who wouldn't run / That animal to death   the white

half white // The black

half white like stars are white / Across a blackness

bigger than   a life is long

Who wouldn't run it just to see it run

If you could make it run until it died

Mulatto

Half donkey and half human being   half horse
Half human being three   halves which end is which
And which the back   for the saddle and which
The fingers for the work   and where the song

Which unrelated to the body pass-
es through the body and that body is
Made more or less   a human body the
Singer's the listener's the listener

Can't help but feel nostalgic and a lit-
tle scandalized half   donkey with its star-
tling hair attached   somehow to something living
Touch it it isn't   smooth like real hair

And every child can sing   and knows the songs

And you will recognize yourself in the singing
And they will sing for any audience
And saddle both   the horse and rider sing

The horse   sings with its back sings   with its fin-
gers and the singing is   not in its eyes
Which are an animal's   not in its hair
Which isn't real   not in its eyes which are

Not real   but only in the body working
And makes the body human working you
Will recognize yourself in the singing   you
Will not recognize yourself in the songs

Niggers on TV

Grew up in Texas 13505
Broadmeade I still   remember the address
And 258-9968 my tele-
phone number not   the area code a yellow

Brick house I hadn't seen the movie but
I knew my house was special from the col-
or of the bricks   it didn't match the other
Houses on the street   I didn't match the neighbors

Darker especially   in the sun I did-
n't think   darker could tan I tanned and knew my
Mother was white   and saw her every month
And didn't see my father didn't want

To didn't   even know his name and didn't

Know he was black not   really and my white

Grandfather hated him and usually

Niggers all niggers except some football play-

ers liked   to watch them run   but they were nig-

gers when they spoke   and niggers when they laughed

At nigger jokes   and niggers when I tried

To look like niggers on tv   on Broad-

meade nobody but me   was niggers and

The Cosby Show   and nobody my grand-

father who raised me let me and my grand-

mother who raised me watch them dance   my grand-

mother who raised me   loved to dance and on-

ly danced with me I only saw her ev-

er dance with me I never saw her dance

But we   watched and we danced   together moved

In time together   with the niggers as

If both of us   were seeing the same thing

MULATTO

Grew up in Texas the only one in school
The only mule   in Round Rock not in Round Rock
As much in Austin as in Round Rock but
Not in between the   only mule at the school

Across the street but there was one black girl
And one black boy much   older boy forgot
Him but the girl   called me a nigger let
The white boys touch the breasts she didn't have

The white boys licked the breasts she didn't have
In second grade   transferred in second grade
From private school a Lutheran school I was
Younger the youngest   boy in the second grade

The white boys licked her breasts   it was a game

It had a name and that was how I knew
It was a game   someone had given it
A name and the white boys were doing it

A white boy named it that   was what it was
And did the thing he named anonymous-
ly while the other   white boys watched from the line
I got in line   and all the white boys saw

There was a nigger in the line   a mule
But none of them could tell   and the one black girl
Called me a nigger made   the white boys laugh
One of us had to save the other one

Mulatto

Neither one otherness nor   the other not
Any not any   every any none
Enjoying every advantage of his par-
entage ran fast and thought and danced and wrote

Not one the same as none   and not the oth-
er less than nothing taller and was black
As anything   a walking nothingness
The less he wore the more I felt like noth-

ing we went skinny-dipping swimming hole
A swimming hole and faster swimmer we
Went skinny-dipping friends of every rac-
es and no Catholics   in the swimming hole

And spoke as well as me and me I spoke

As well as anybody   else I knew
Though everybody else I knew spoke bet-
ter came from more   and didn't have my luck

And he and me and he the other one
One black one white one neither one we were
The best of friends of every races not
This nor the other otherness the on-

ly otherness allowed exalted and
Examined not   too close examined not
Too far away examined taught to read
Disposable but tugged at the heart his hands

His father's hands his palms at least as skin-
colored as anybody's not a gar-
ish pink   skin-colored like his father's palms
The other one my   children are quadroons

He had a sister married her I would
Have married her we would have run away
Together but the north does not exist
And where could we have gone I have three chil-

dren no one anytime says much since eve-
rybody knows   but people like to talk
And people talk and people will and we
Don't talk about it but we are in love

She would have married me if I had asked
But she's her brother's sister more than she's
Her father's daughter says she doesn't need
To marry me and what's the use of ask-

ing doesn't need a wedding ring to raise
A white man's children   smarter yes I think
Stronger than other children even such

Attenuated blood one drop a horse

With a man's head is not a horse   and not
A man it is a myth and I have seen one
It is a myth and I have seen one in
The woods behind my true love's wooden cot-

tage wooden room   I would have married her
But where could we have gone it is a myth
And I have seen one in the water swim-
ming in the water in the woods in the dirt-

y water in the swimming hole a myth
Mule with a black boy's head I saw it swim-
ming it was not   my child I'm sure it was not
A quarter not a whole and not a half

5

Housekeeping

1

And after even   less my mother's real / Mother weighed after even less my moth-
er came out   small I came out one
Month late and dead and even
through drugs / My mother saw and fainted

but not small / My mother hadn't smoked at all her moth- / er had
to keep the baby small her own
Weight down I came out upside down   and legs
First and her husband was a handsome boy
And tried to kill her twice

he tried   to kill her in the car / He tried to flip the car   he parked the car
On railroad tracks and beat her
till she could- / n't crawl away
and then he drove away   / Her real
father he was as handsome as he loved

2

And after less   and even less   she less she   sheing less / She lost

weight during weighed less at the end   / I didn't start

driving until I was

Twenty and that   was how she told the story   / Until she couldn't crawl away

And smoked   and drank   she never said she didn't know

This was the fifties   even then they knew

She never said she would have done things differently

And after   nurses walked

Her to the incubator   and she saw me / Alive for the first time my / Mother she thought I looked

Like a machine

and love was not the thing she thought it was

and my / Mother was eighteen   and a dropout and

3

Her mother looked   just like a young Elizabeth

Taylor and she was twenty-four   / He was her third

husband she went / After him with a butcher knife

Was after he   had tried to flip the car / Was after he

had beaten her

Until she couldn't crawl

and after he

after the knife / Decided   they should get divorced

But kept her figure with

My mother in her belly / By putting nothing in her body / But smoke

by suffocating her my   mother even then

And kept her figure even then   / And loving her her real

mother

but how to be in charge   of all the beauty in the home

No Country

Most otherwise most beautiful most beau-
tiful the same   and otherwise and bright
Here bright here beautiful   most walking though
Most moved   and were I not a patriot

Most walking through wave walking through the o-
cean loses   every step its body she
Most walking through   a crowded room   or in
Public and were she not each injury

Most walking disembodied through the air
Most watched looked after   watched and what
Eye looks and doesn't take most beautiful
And what eye looks and gives   what wave is part

Of the ocean it makes   visibly an ocean

Most walking through if no man loves his country
Because no country has a body or
What country gives   and does not take the body

Most otherwise and bright here beautiful
And from one city to the next espe-
cially a train built specially one cit-
y to the next   most walking every step

From one compartment to the next she loses
Her body   crowded   and which step is part
Forward or backward   of the motion of
The train   and were I not a patriot

I wouldn't look   and bright here bright here beauti-
ful otherwise   no country loves the body

Pietà

And *yes* the body and   the body most / Without   *yes*   *yes*

her legs and if   / She stood you said   *monstrous*

and *yes*   / And if

she stood her body standing least   / The Lord

to love the body first   destroys the body

And if she stood her body standing least

her body / *Yes*   and *yes*   *monstrous* and her   face a child's / Face

and her son's   body a child's

Body the Lord   to love the body first

Gave her a son who could not love her   *yes*

Monstrous the Lord

to love the body   punishes the body / *Yes*   with the body

The Lord   with the body and   *monstrous* with love   / And *yes*

the body most   refusing *yes*   to stand

resists

Mosaic

Some are diagonal what would she have thought
Though most are vertical or horizontal
She would have thought we do not think alike
But what would she have thought   a photograph
Mosaic of her face one photograph
Repeated changed   sometimes her hair is black
And sometimes red but not   the way it in real
Life was not ever red   not ever black and not

Ever the blond it is in the other pho-
tographs and   what would she have thought she would
Have thought I do not notice him and if
I do we do not think alike   but what
Would she have thought if she had seen herself
Not ever blond but blond not ever what
She was in a mosaic   some of the pho-

tographs diagonal not straight   or would

She not have thought of that at all would she
Have thought I do not notice him or could
I not have come   being too young before
She died   if she had lived she might have no-
ticed me   I would have been a child if she
Had lived a few more years   a toddler or
A schoolboy strange to see and she might know
My face now if she saw it if she had

Mausoleum

In summer   in a cold month Februar-

y spring in August we   drove to her grave

Grandmother you and I your mother's grave

In the mausoleum in a cemeter-

y full   of ordinary graves   in the mau-

soleum not a grave   I didn't know

Grandmother then what you knew now   I know

Burning a body is cheaper than a fu-

neral a grave   now that we've had to burn

Grandmother my   mother and I your bod-

y and   the poor are buried in the wall

And buried you   grandmother in the wall

Remember   when you would inherit grand-

mother the earth   first you must break through the stone

[Grandmother O my mother]

Grandmother O my mother
Will lose her house in the spring
She doesn't want another
House   but she wants your things

To stay in the family
She can't say what they are
Grandmother   O a stray
Cat and some furniture

And things I wouldn't know
Or ever guess you had
Grandmother O   you're more
Familiar to me dead

Than you in the last slow months

Of your Alzheimer's were

Grandmother   I don't want

The cat   the furniture

The strangeness of the face

You couldn't   when I came

Grandmother O quite place

Is now my living name

6

Are Roses Are

And we divorced in the bud and green of May

Bird-flower and hummingbird

-flower bee-flower / Drone-flower   and buzzing not

only the wings / But every part the stamen and the root

And every part the morning and the day / The day and day

-flower and the white flowers

Ghost orchids and vanilla orchids long / Dry shadows on the marsh

black shadows not

Reflections on the marsh   of the orchids in the marsh

Bee-flower drone-flower   the shadows

swaying and / The buzzing flowers swaying and

The shadows swaying   as the buzzing flowers / Swayed in the wind

and with the marsh / And in

the night the night

-flowers are roses are

In the bud and green

vanilla   orchids ghost / Orchids   the bees a kind of lemon candy

Not natural but the best

part of the fruit

Because the tongue begins to die if used   / We spoke our vows and signed for the divorce

Because the tongue begins to die   we placed

Bitter and sharp   things on our tongues in the morn- / ing of the day

we married and we placed / Bitter things sharp

things in our mouths

the morning we divorced / The bees

a kind of butterscotch   on the hot- / test days of August and the swarm

-ing gnats small clumps of mucus caught in the throat

And we divorced

in May the bud and green the / Heat of the marsh

the only sound

The marsh made

and the buzzing

flowers / And hummingbird

the water though   was cool

And every part of the water was the day   / And we

and you and I stood at the edge / Of the park   and moths were gathering the light

From the streetlight gathering

and car- / rying the light away returning and / The honey was the light

the marsh in the mid- / dle of the park   at the edge of the park a row

Of cars at the edge of the park   and the men wait- / ing in the cars

for the men in the cars to call

Them to the park   to carry them to lay / Them down in the park   and we

stood at the edge / Waiting for something else

the light   was honey when moths flew

Away with the light   and every part

of the moths / Was day   and we divorced in May and spring   / Our son

was almost five and couldn't talk

Our son was almost five

and if I died / In the house   and he was left alone in the house

And he can't feed himself   some mornings I

Wake and my fingertips are numb I wake

And almost I   think I will almost clean the house

And in the morning he is singing in his bed   / No

words a high-pitched moan   and runs out cry

-ing flowers flowers crying   birds in the trees / Outside the window crying thinks the birds

are in the house

No end to the self

No words for how it does not end

And we

divorced in the marsh the flower named

Vanilla and the flavor on the tongue

Our son in the morning singing in his bed / Among the cattails and the tall grass

we / Stood at the edge and then were standing

in the marsh / The moths

made honey of the light to make

Honey they left the light they brought

the honey back / Or died in the light the light

itself too sweet to leave   / The moths

a kind of tissue paper on the tongue / And we are standing in the marsh

Waiting and I can't tell you what I see   / And we

and you see something else

we did / Not choose a life that could be changed

And we must change our lives

7

Continuing

Dear Lord if this   is what I make
of my / Body why give me Lord a body if
It might have been   like all creation beautiful
Why give it Lord to me
that even now / Survives the fattening   and the disease
And even now I treasure why
Give me a body Lord   and love
In the body for the body love and love
Lord calls / Me from my body Lord   and love is no
release   / But more compacting more
Body O Lord if this is what I make
Of love   if this is how I break / My body
which even now I treasure
for / Continuing
if this is what I love   if this is how

Crows

Dear Lord-And-Spring   and spring the trees / Are raw with birds   are Lord green
hearts on trunks / Beating and Lord
giant hearts the spring is
Lord / That season

and an animal
all heart and bone / And nothing Lord and Lord You fill
the nothing in   / And spring is most like You
and black / Birds in the trees black

arteries / The color of   the thing beneath the skin / Is not the color of the skin
the color of the birds / In the trees
is not the color of the leaves / And Lord the sound of their wings
is the sound of the leaves   / The living thing

in the heart is not the heart

The crows in the heart

Scavenge in the heart   / Lord which was full

and welcomed them

[Lord Mouth dear]

Lord Mouth dear   Tongue dear Only-Pierceable-
Parts to what now shall I compare Thee Lord
I am a lonely man   I do not see
My children often   to a summer's day
To autumn   Lord   Thou art more peaceable
Less difficult to leave to   die in more
Relenting though the sun does set   in the sea
Shall I compare these things   to Thee Lord my
Daughter when she was thirteen months old walked
My son when he was fifteen months old walked
I did not see   my son and daughter walk
Although the sun does set   in the sea Lord dear
Heart to what now   shall I compare Thee dear
Father who art   more lovely and less dear

[Dear Once-Incarnate-Silence]

Dear Once-Incarnate-   Silence dear

Lord if I leave Your table full

Who hungers in my place I see

My place is full dear   Can't-We-All-

Just-Get-Along   dear Every-King

You are the city burning in

Which I am burned Lord if I am

Not who   is burning I smell skin

Burning Lord I would choose the fire

To praise You from the fire if I

Could see a way   out of the fire

Lord if I had a choice if my

Mother and father and my son

And daughter were not burning here

Lord I would choose the fire for love

Of You   if those I love were spared

[LORD OF THE HOPELESS]

Lord of the hopeless also dear   Hat-Soaked
Pole-In-The-Canal and Red-Tie Father   Son
And Holy Ghost not   in that order break
The rottenness of those who torture one
Of Thy least wrath-deserving exiles me
Not   wholly undeserving   no   but some
And isn't it the some that counts with Thee
O   Gondola also as the trees pass warm
Overhead I   can close my eyes and they
Are almost not   burning and this is any
River to the sea O   Lord I do not say
Release me call me home forgive my many
Sins I say Lord forgive my torturers
Who hate my faults   as if my faults were theirs

[Lord God Lord Basket Lord]

Lord God Lord Basket Lord   gather them in
My sisters brothers father mother her
Mother who died   the day before her birth-
day yesterday and my   great-uncle who
Wanted his sister's money   none of us
Have money Lord or ever had   the dis-
appointed and the generous   the scru-
pulous the criminals   the criminals with
Scruples Lord gather them the wives and liars
Husbands and liars gather them the hon-
est ones   and the ones who married well Lord Mi-
grant-Worker pick them gather them Lord al-
so those they love   who maybe are not me
And those who love You though not always well

8 (NEW POEMS)

The Insect Wife and Husband

We married in an overgrowth of bulbs
Wide fields of water lilies and low hills
Shipped over from another continent
Brick by soft brick we   married on a boat

A cradle   rocking on the sea floor skull
And crossbones flags torn loose by the currents filled
The sky-blue water overhead as con-
tinents drifted   and slowly we were lost

We married in a basket of dry leaves
We were the insect   wife and husband hid-
den in a basket of dry leaves   ourselves

Dry leaves we lived still   not once noisy lives
Until a windstorm scooped us from our bed
One storm now separates and carries us

Our Hearts Were New

We married in a jar with holes in the lid
We were not insects   but we were both small
And had glass skin almost invisible
And graphite hearts that made black marks inside
Our skin our   hearts both looked like thumbprints on
A mirror from the beating of our hearts
Irregularly beating   smudges not
Beautiful hearts not human or cartoon
Hearts but our arms and legs   our faces and
Our hearts were human   and the jar was hu-
man was   a part of us no part of us
Was human in the world but in the glass
Jar every part was our   hearts pounded hard
Our hearts   were new and their black stains were new

The Math

We married in one hundred dirty hooves

Which means no   animals were missing legs

But some were missing legs we married in

The math so probably twenty-six may-

be twenty-seven animals some moved

More slowly but   not in a natural way

Than others some   were sleeping some were beg-

ging some were paralyzed   some of the an-

imals had been   back from the war a long

Time and were ready to forget the war

Some of the animals had fought a short-

er war off   to the side or in the wrong

Country and wanted to remember sort-

ing them out took   another war   we married in the second war in the second war

Birds fought   birds fought each other for the an-

imals and didn't leave   marks where they fell

We married in one hundred dirty hooves

Except the dirt was blurry here and there

Where the birds fell the animals removed

The hollow bodies of the birds as soon

As almost before they fell   the animals

Dragged them so   quickly off the dirt was smeared

The war belonged   to the animals the birds

Could fight could die and   thanks   but leave no trace

We married in the shadow of a hawk

Killing a hawk   sometimes the shadow looked

Like one giant bird sometimes   it looked like us

The Long Scream

We married in a different kind of war
In every war we married in we mar-
ried in the same war every morning we
Woke in the war   in an unchanging bed and
With sometimes just a thumb or clump of hair
Sometimes a living body you or me
Asleep still next to me or you we were
Asleep we living humans next to the dead and
Couldn't be told apart except   we living
Emitted a low hum the hum   was cut
With screams eventually a long scream put
Us humming long to sleep in   climbed more violent
Screams louder   dead the low hum   stopped we living
Slept in a bed of screams and human silence

When the Doctors Came

1

We married in the branches of a tall
Tree a deciduous tree in the summer in
The block of forest at the end of the street
Not high enough to see beyond the leaves
Not close enough to the ground to jump   the leaves
Shook green and thick in gusts inside but not

Outside the branches in the branches in
The forest in the summer in the fall
In the forest of the summer mostly ever-
greens among evergreens our son was born
As gusts in the branches   stripped the leaves from the branches
And left us three   in the open air in the branches

And when the doctors came the doctors came
Clinging to needles carried from the ever-
greens in the fur of squirrels and the doc-
tors came curled up in balls in the hearts of pearls
Glued to a lost bracelet the doctors came
Riding seeds in bird shit down

2

our son / Was born as gusts of wind
but when the doc- / tors came to treat him he
for the first time / Stopped
being wind and for the first time had a physical / Body he stopped
surrounding us

And slept instead
in the branches in his cra- / dle and the doctors treated him for years
And were so small they after years

Became a thin   layer of dust

Covering him

                    taking his shape

a mask and uniform / Of dust

taking his shape away

My Grandmother Married a White Supremacist and Became a White Supremacist

We filed the papers at a hydrant my
Grandmother painted over over and
Over again the hydrant in her front
Yard at the edge of her front   yard bright col-
ors   faces bodies wearing brightly col-
ored clothes with faces and always   the cit-
y someone   working for the city found
Out and repainted painted over my
Grandmother never went to college   art
School but she won a scholarship to art
School but she married young   her husband was
A painter went to college painted wom-
en nudes and rocks the rocks rock-gray the wom-
en brown like rocks   from which fresh water flows

The Tulip Garden

And we divorced in spring the tulip garden

A field of tulips and a field of wheat / A field of wheat a field of wheat

the road   / From Silverton to Salem and the road

From Salem to Mount Angel and the road

From Silverton to Mount

Angel were not / The same road

and the tulips changed and did / Not change

the changing colors everywhere in

The same place everywhere and each

color there its own world / And separate from the other col- / ors a

red world a purple world / The tulips

changed and driving

to return- / ing from   we glanced at those bright

things we loved together

And that was how we loved each other

In the Helicopter Seeds

And we divorced in snow and in the following

Spring in the helicopter seeds

That were not beautiful   until they fell   / As helicopters are most useful for

The way they land

And we divorced   in flowers and in the summer / Flowers blossom in the summer

and the lil- / y on the water is a blossoming cloud

And if the koi in the water   left the water

For the blossom they would suffocate and would / Leave

if they knew

but not for the flower

and we divorced in fall and the next winter / The days seemed warmer

When gray clouds blocked the sun

as if the sun could burn   unseen

As if the sun could shine and not be ours

In the Mountains

And we divorced in the mountains and the stars   / No clearer in the mountains
and we saw / The stars
clearer in the mountains and the wa- / ter rolling

down the mountain was the mountain
Destroyed by water and the water roll- / ing down
the mountain was the water un-

able to penetrate the rock we did
Not choose a life that could be changed   and we
Must change our lives

and we divorced in the mountains   / Where high in the mountains animals
We wouldn't recognize as living
in / The mountains   and impossible

at sea / Level watched us stalked us were

Ready to kill us

if we tried to trap them where they lived

After the Hearing

And we divorced in hallways and in strangers' clothes / And rushing forward
rushing backward ei-
ther way
always away

Rushing away lean strangers guiding us
In strangers' clothes and rushing
for the ex-   / it each
afraid the other one   would get out first O   O / Rushing

one hallway to the next the next
Sometimes in the opposite direction no
Corners between the two
and I do

not   / Remember turning strangers guid- / ing us away

the strangers guided by

Strangers who looked like us   from far away

And from behind

But couldn't have been us those strangers

howling   pounding on the gate

The Glacier Divorced the Water

And we divorced in ice a block of ice
A drifting block of ice a glacier not
A cube that kind of block a mostly sunk-
en pyramid   the hidden kind and we
Divorced in sunlight   drifting south the ice
Daily more quickly disappearing but
The sunlight couldn't reach us at the dark
Center of the glacier   underwater the

Glacier I should have said not us divorced
In sunlight drifting south the glacier it
Divorced the water meaning it went back
To being liquid water not a block
Of ice   and we went back to drowning at
Last   free of the deathly and preserving ice

Afterword

Shane McCrae

Long prose in front of me, I start poems, and finish poems, and then start other poems, but not this prose about poems I wrote ten years ago, eleven years ago, some even twelve, but about me, my childhood, thirty to forty-two years ago, and even before then, time before time, before I was kidnapped, which I talk about and I'll talk about in the long prose I'm not writing, but should. When I can choose to write a poem I'll write a poem rather than do almost anything, family in another sphere, time with them, but rather than almost anything else. And most of the time since I started writing the poems that became *Mule,* I've been able to write when I've wanted to, though not always well or ever well. Mostly that's because I figured out who I am as a writer by writing *Mule,* and that, so far, has freed me to write (though I'm conscious that freedom could disappear at any moment).

Technique calls words into being, whatever one's technique might be. Before I wrote the poems in *Mule,* my technique had been consciously borrowed from other poets because I wanted my poems to sound like their poems: Priscilla Becker, whose poems I loved more than anybody's when I was getting my MFA and just before, and whose technique I worked the hardest to imitate, and John Ashbery, who, whenever I read his poems, immediately overwhelmed me into wanting to write poems like his, which prevented me from thoroughly absorbing his technique; that is to say, I never sat with his technique, but wrote poems according to what I could perceive on its surface. But I had studied traditional versification when I was an undergraduate and just before, and every so often a sonnet would struggle its way out, usually over-punctuated but also usually at least semi-successfully metered and rhymed.

While I was borrowing techniques, poems came to me infrequently. My desire to write poems that would sound like the poems of others prevented me from writing any other kinds of poems, and the imitations I every few weeks managed were difficult to get out, snuck as they were from the houses of others.

Eventually, after I had finished my MFA and began pursuing a JD, and thanks mostly to the frankness of Garth Greenwell, which was a world to me—at the time he was a graduate student in the English program at Harvard—and the attention of Jorie Graham, which was a world to me, I decided to stop trying (consciously, at least) to imitate other poets, and in fact to change most of how I wrote poems. I decided, in other words, to change my technique.

The changes I made, I made in an effort to, as I conceived the effort then, do the opposite of everything I had been doing when I wrote poems, but I didn't understand the effects of the changes, with regard to the act of composition itself, until much later. I stopped using punctuation, which encouraged me to write more quickly (partially because doing so encouraged me to write a faster line). I started employing repetition and non-standard syntax, which discouraged me from untroubled linearity. And I stopped writing free verse altogether, which lessened my anxiety about the forms my poems should take—rather than a void into which to write, I now had form. Almost immediately—as soon as I got the hang of what I was doing; it might have been two or three days—I started writing a poem, beginning to end, pretty much every day, sometimes two or three a day. Since then, so long as I've had time to write—some days being too busy to do anything other than what the day itself requires—that pace hasn't slowed down. As of this writing, I've had fourteen, in a month fifteen, years of this undeserved happiness.

That's how I started writing the poems that became *Mule*.

A few months later, worrying my poems would soon start to bore people—I was in Jorie's workshop at the time, and so could assume, luxuriously, that people would be reading what I wrote—I decided I had to add something new to what I was already doing. I remember sitting down at my desk, it was foldable card table, the legs were foldable, from Target, one day after workshop, and thinking, "What if I could write poems that were simultaneously traditionally metrical poems and free verse poems?" And though some part of my mind dismissed the idea—how could one do such a thing?—another part of my mind considered it, and it wasn't long, a few minutes, maybe, until I had figured out how to write what had seemed just a few minutes before, and, in an abstract way, for years before then, an impossible poem. Years ago, it was about two years after I figured out how to write that kind of poem, I wrote a paragraph for *No Tell Motel* explaining my technique:

> I don't write free verse poems—mostly because I can't. But I am interested in the musical effects achievable with free verse. Several of these poems [along with this paragraph, *No Tell Motel* published a few poems later included in *Mule*] are the results of my attempts to create a meter that is simultaneously formal and free, and to think, for musical purposes, at the level of the verse paragraph rather than the line. As a consequence, the metrically important unit is the verse paragraph—e.g., a traditional sonnet has seventy feet (5 feet per line x 14 lines), and since what matters when writing in this way is the total number of feet (and, of course, the poems do rhyme, though some of the rhymes are very slant, and don't follow a regular pattern), individual line lengths can vary, so long as the thing has 70 feet at the end. "In No Place," for instance, is made up of three sonnets, or 210 feet. Where a line "ends" metrically is denoted by a "/" if that point falls anywhere other than the actual end of a line, and generally where each new line "begins" metrically is denoted with a capital letter (the only exception being when a line begins mid-word).

That's how I continued writing the poems that became *Mule*.

One's first book is and remains the only book one ever writes, and also vanishes from one's mind—at the very least, it vanishes from one's catalogue of things one has made, or things with which, if "made" is too strong a word, it feels too strong, one has been involved. Largely, this is because, more so than with regard to any of one's subsequent books, one perceives its merits, and especially its faults, differently from the ways others perceive its merits and faults—the gap has longer to get wide. In a month, *Mule* will have been published ten years ago, but to me it is wild still, but maybe it would be more correct to say it has long ago crossed some boundary beyond which I am no longer capable of seeing it right, of knowing whether it is wild or tame. At the time, I put everything I had into it, not knowing it would keep what I gave it, not knowing it would run away, though I knew it was wild. But what was everything I had? A changed life, just beginning.

New York City, December 2020

ACKNOWLEDGMENTS

Boundless gratitude to the writers who were generous enough to help me with this book, without whom it would not be: Katie Ford, Jorie Graham, Victoria Chang, and Melissa McCrae.

And boundless gratitude also to everyone at the Cleveland State University Poetry Center, especially Michael Dumanis, Amy Freels, and Krysia Orlowski, and to the editors and staffs of the following journals, in which some of the poems first appeared, sometimes in different versions:

African American Review:	"Mulatto" [Grew up in Texas the only one in school...]
Agni:	"In the Garden of the Ghosts of the Garden" "Mulatto" [Half donkey and half human being...]
The American Poetry Review:	"Horses Running Fast" "Mulatto" [Neither one otherness nor...]
Anglican Theological Review:	"[Dear Once-Incarnate-Silence]"
Colorado Review:	"After the Diagnosis"
Effing Magazine:	"Singing" "[We married on a battlefield]"
The Harvard Advocate:	"[We married in a thorax]"
Image:	"[Lord Mouth dear]" "[Lord of the hopeless]"
Kenyon Review Online:	"Continuing" "Sightseeing"

Mantis:	"A Dancer There" "Are Roses Are" "Internal Horses" (as "Nicholas Rode Internal Horses") "[We married in the front yard]"
New Orleans Review:	"The Boy Calls Twilight" "The Cardinal Is the Marriage Bird" "[Lord God Lord Basket Lord]" "Mausoleum" "Recovery" "[We married in a taxi]" "[We married in his belly]" "[We married on a speeding train]"
No Tell Motel:	"[Grandmother O my mother]" "In No Place" "The Survives"
Octopus:	"No Country"
West Branch:	"Pietà" "That's Entertainment"

"The Cardinal Is the Marriage Bird" and "That's Entertainment" were reprinted on *Poetry Daily.*

"Pietà" also appears in *The Best American Poetry 2010.*

Some of these poems appear in a chapbook, *One Neither One,* published by Octopus Books.

RECENT CLEVELAND STATE UNIVERSITY POETRY CENTER PUBLICATIONS

Edited by Caryl Pagel & Hilary Plum

POETRY

World'd Too Much: The Selected Poetry of Russell Atkins ed. Kevin Prufer and Robert E. McDonough
Advantages of Being Evergreen by Oliver Baez Bendorf
Dream Boat by Shelley Feller
My Fault by Leora Fridman
Orient by Nicholas Gulig
Twice There Was A Country by Alen Hamza
Age of Glass by Anna Maria Hong
In One Form to Find Another by Jane Lewty
50 Water Dreams by Siwar Masannat
daughterrarium by Sheila McMullin
The Bees Make Money in the Lion by Lo Kwa Mei-en
Residuum by Martin Rock
Festival by Broc Rossell
Sun Cycle by Anne Lesley Selcer
Arena by Lauren Shapiro
Bottle the Bottles the Bottles the Bottles by Lee Upton

ESSAYS

I Liked You Better Before I Knew You So Well by James Allen Hall
A Bestiary by Lily Hoang
Codependence by Amy Long
The Leftovers by Shaelyn Smith

TRANSLATIONS

Scorpionic Sun by Mohammed Khaïr-Eddine, translated by Conor Bracken
I Burned at the Feast: Selected Poems of Arseny Tarkovsky translated by Philip Metres and Dimitri Psurtsev

For a complete list of titles visit www.csupoetrycenter.com

VICTORIA CHANG's latest poetry book is *OBIT,* which was named a *New York Times Notable Book* and a *TIME* best book of the year. The book received an Anisfield-Wolf Book Award, the PEN Voelcker Award, and the *Los Angeles Times* Book Prize. It was also longlisted for a National Book Award and named a finalist for the National Book Critics Circle Award and the Griffin Poetry Award. She has written four other poetry books and several children's books. She has received a Guggenheim Fellowship, a Sustainable Arts Foundation Fellowship, the Poetry Society of America's Alice Fay Di Castagnola Award, a Pushcart Prize, a Lannan Residency Fellowship, and a Katherine Min MacDowell Colony Fellowship. She lives in Los Angeles and is the Program Chair of Antioch's Low-Residency MFA Program.

SHANE MCCRAE's most recent books are *Sometimes I Never Suffered,* shortlisted for the T. S. Eliot Prize, and *The Gilded Auction Block,* both published by Farrar, Straus and Giroux. He has received a Lannan Literary Award, a Whiting Writer's Award, an Anisfield-Wolf Book Award, and fellowships from the Guggenheim Foundation, the National Endowment for the Arts, and the New York Foundation for the Arts. He lives in New York City and teaches at Columbia University.